Winter Garden

The Gerald Cable Book Award Series

Winter Garden

Robert Hunter Jones

Silverfish Review Press
Eugene, Oregon

Published by
Silverfish Review Press
PO Box 3541
Eugene, OR 97403
www.silverfishreviewpress.com

Distributed by
Small Press Distribution
800-869-7553
spd@spdbooks.org
www.spdbooks.org

Library of Congress Cataloging-in-Publication Data

Names: Jones, Robert Hunter.
Title: Winter garden / Robert Hunter Jones.
Description: First edition. | Eugene, OR : Silverfish Review Press, 2016.
Identifiers: LCCN 2015048998 | ISBN 9781878851673 (pbk. : alk. paper)
Classification: LCC PS3610.O627675 A6 2016 | DDC 811/.6--dc23
LC record available at http://lccn.loc.gov/2015048998

9 8 7 6 5 4 3 2 First Printing
Printed in the United States of America

Contents

For my mother, Severn Jones,
and in memory of my father,
William Hunter Jones, 1923–1994.

Finally, to Jan, Branson, and Delaney,
for the place to stand.

" 'They are our people, yours and mine,
all of us,' he said.
'In every storm I hear them pass.' "

"People Who Went by in Winter"
—William Stafford

Winter Garden

Exact Directions of Light

The sky is made of accidents, the moon
just one of them. Ask the storied firmament
what the North Star means and you begin
to see the problem. We were young enough

to credit our chances of mapping the night
with meaning, but owned too the unlikely
nature of chance and how it made of circumstance
the necessary shapes to shut the darkness up.

She said, "Stars shine in each direction equally
or do not shine at all." With nothing to hand
I scratched this in low tide mud, then waited
by the fire until the moon shifted it away.

We climbed back uphill in darkness and drove
north on Highway 1. I don't recall her name,
only the sweep of light just far enough ahead
to convince us of direction. Memory is night

redacted by the gravity of time—the contours
of her face glimpsed by dash light, downshifting
into the sharpest corners while the incessant
surf worried stones smooth far below.

Childhood

Forty-nine years ago we folded a bike in half
by dropping it seventy feet from Tenmile Bridge
onto the old highway guard rail far below.

We needed gravity to justify itself. We bent it to better shape
then carried the bike to the center of the bridge and let it
fall into the creek below. Heraclites never learned

to ride a bike, and history is vague on the question
of aquatic skill. Few certainties attain, but one is that
the folded bike is still under all of it. Don't cast your nets
there, for what you pull back feeds no one.

Breakfast Included

Light enters
by way of my timid desires.
Gradually intensified by its need
of horizons, it creates the world.

I kneel. The earth lifts itself
to my mouth. I rise then
like some rooted thing into its own
appetite. The world has chosen teeth.

I gnaw the songs of birds, chew
the light from flowers and leaves.
I scratch through dirt to gulp
the secret meat of worms.

I devour my own
mouth—the tender lips
give way to a long smile
that eats the tongue behind it.

Only teeth remain. Let them
grind themselves to dust
and disperse as luminous seed
into a universe yearning

for a new source of wonder:
Light defines some far horizon.
Hunger rises.

The Bullfrog

—for Ed, after your letter

1.

I acquired the habit early
of making up problems that didn't occur
naturally in my life, as though
some imagined richness there
would not rise on its own from the mud.

I might have heard latent warning
in the hoarse susurrations of his songs
had I known then how the future
listens to us traveling toward it.

October once meant
an even mix of hard rain
and clear cold nights, when the stars
seemed wet and close, and the sky
held the curves of my face to itself.

It is quieter now at night, and drier.
I am older, full of the little agonies
that follow like afternoon shadows
long after actual events.

2.

Years now I've tried to tell this
straight, how you were patient, inclusive,
destined like all of your kind to suffer.
That you came one Sunday to visit me alone
was a gift I knew would never be repeated.

I only wanted to show you something,
some rare moment to separate myself
from the others. In this grip, I took
the flimsy bow, my one dull arrow,
and marshaled our party along
the edge of the ditch.

I spread bunches of cut-grass
to show you the clusters of frog eggs
huddled there, each like a gathering of eyes
suspended in water, waiting
for bodies to look from.

We found him poised to jump
but unmoving.

What I remember most—after
sending the arrow again and again
through the loose accepting bag
of his body—is the sense of you
behind me, watching, sickened
as I was, while the frog himself
seemed unchanged, even calm.

When I shot for the head, wanting only
to end this, the arrow jumped back, and his eyes
turned milky. Into the small round holes
the arrow left, the old world
drained away.

3.

Casual is the root word
of casualty. The unmeant act
that opens a random path leading
to the rest of our lives. The cracked

mirror throwing its years
of bad luck and distortions
back into faces already lined like
palms clenched in the womb.

When I part the grass, there
by the water waits the bullfrog.

pinus contorta

Trimming shore pine along the edge
of the field, I work through the strange light
of these shortest days while high winds off the dunes
blow down rain warm and fine enough to breathe.

The pines huff and surge. Named for a willingness
to haggle, they colonize soils so coarse the word
is a misnomer, building them from the slough
of their own bodies. These severed limbs are musical

when cut to length and tossed into a pile.
Green and sap-heavy, they must cure a year
in open air before they feed the woodstove.

A study of darkness and light reveals wounds
grown over, lean years. No grudge records itself
here, only a pure acceptance of being.

My Father Drinking Water

A delicate tipping back of the head,
mouth opened carefully, a graceful
pouring motion that revealed a certain
fragility, a tentative relationship to thirst

quite unlike the way I'd seen him
put whiskey back. None of that
grim certainty that looked like
fate finding its way into its own

bland darkness. Twenty years have passed
and I realize, glancing at what's left
of him in the mirror, how rarely I observed
the kind of drinking that did not kill him.

He was a man thirst reached for, and he filled himself—
not gently but completely. I might have offered
what the oasis can the lost. Now I'm afraid
I looked the other way.

Saying a World

So in this room, near the window
of broken light, we sit and talk quietly.
She measures her words, intervals of
silence, sound, silence. I wait out
the sentences, watch them form

in the space between us, coupling
like cars of a soft careful train. She says
if she has intelligence, it is the basic kind,
the type that builds houses, puts food
in the mouths of the hungry. I laugh,

rationing my need. It has cost her to come
this far. I want to tell her she is well off, that
my mind is of another variety, much like a sky
with no earth beneath it. But I say nothing.
I sit with her in a room where light

runs us through. Slowly she speaks a floor
under our feet, then a new door leading out.
Soon she'll say a hand to draw the door
open. There is the fact of this light, how it
opens us. We will leave here together.

Games of Risk

A letter to Pete Carlson
Anchorage, 1985

I write from the long missing heart
of the far country. Only four nights back
we had the world at our fingertips, spread out
in a tent on the wide fields below Sand Ridge.

She was lovely—a beginner, she claimed, and we
coddled her in a way more arrogant than kind.
In the end the dice leapt from her fingers.
One by one she fed us our hearts fresh

from their cages. Mine, as you know, is not
a necessary organ. Still, I miss its rhythm.
I am sick and hungry, and at night the world
grows unbearably cold. I survive eating ants

and chewing the bark from snow-bent saplings.
I sleep in the sun, and the big moon keeps me moving
at night. Now it is just a question of time. The abyss
that opens below me is as fathomless as a woman's

real intentions. The world is far bigger than the board
allows us to believe. Each night the fires of her armies
burn nearer. I hear singing through the trees. This note
I trust to the wind and hope it finds you. Remember me

when your power is massed at the borders, when
you've a set in hand and a wild card down. Think of me
while the dice are still kind—running alone in the wilderness,
gnawing at saplings like the legs of young women.

Let me tell you something: the moon is more
necessary than beautiful, a woman's smile
is only teeth, the game is never over, never over,
never over—these words in the wind.

To Sharpen a Pulaski

"All things have come now into their comparisons."
—*Robert Duncan*

At first the file skitters and slides across
years of attempts to introduce an edge.
When it takes, the clean peel of metal
announces the arrival of new possibilities.

It is here that patience weds itself
to love. Most men want the quick edge.
It blunts a tool and cheats the steel
of its natural appetites. A delicately

tapered head bites deep and stays
hungry longer. Work the file gently.
Begin with the shoulders and forgive yourself
all the initial awkwardness. Let the metal

undress itself one luminous stroke
at a time. A reciprocal softness waits
in the steel to reflect a version of your face
you could never have guessed existed.

Thumbnail Sketch

With her almost perfect thumbnail
she split the belly of a seed and looked in.
She knows the names of scattered grasses

alive in pumice soils beneath the cliffs.
Given wind and rain, these names lift themselves
and lean far into their meanings.

But when light this late changes on the cliffs, then
we change too. Those two graceful hemlocks
gesture into a last still dance while the sky
pales into its entire emptiness.

There's nothing left to say. Sometimes words falter
at the edges of moments like these, just beyond reach
in shadows that'll turn any face we dare to recall.

I remember her slowing on the trail
when light was old like this.

She placed a single berry in my palm. Perfect,
it rolled across all the clenched dead ends
of this life, promising the sweetness
summer lets swell from its blossom.

Daddy Leaves Home

They can no longer separate what he is
from his disease. Two weeks, they said.
We are sorry to inform you.

Three days later in a House of Pancakes
she looks down at her plate and hears
a man laugh. What is this? she asks, meaning

the food, the restaurant, this laughter.
It is a fine place for breakfast, she says,
always a wait. She hears the laugh again

and tracks it carefully through all the voices
and gestures, across tables and people
and plates of food, to a man in the corner

and into the cave of his mouth. The laugh
is her father's laugh. What is it doing here,
in another city, in another man's mouth?

She looks with greater care around the room.
What else might have followed her?
She studies faces, listens for inflections

or particular ways of waiting to speak.
She recalls then a dream that recurs: *a child follows*
her father to a door among windows. She knows

he means to speak, but his voice is only light and his face
a window through which it is shining. Beyond the clear pane
the driveway is empty, the old Plymouth gone.

Not Writing Friends

I know there is nothing to say. Our relatives
all died years ago, or hang on, persistent
as colds. Some take on the waiting
like a second job, the empty mailbox
brimming with air worth breathing.

I tilt the blinds and watch the mailman
walk by in white light. The weather
never changes. I wonder now, not writing,
how you feel about long winters, snow in July,
fear aching in your teeth. This business of blood
pulsing in the veins misleads us to great beliefs.

At night, trees stand in themselves,
pointing out stars unhinted by the naked eye.
I mean something else when I say nothing.
Silence, the world's way of breaking
its news, pays our most pressing respects.

Hold this page in moonlight. Let it show
empty as a snowfield glowing. Mail it back.

Managed Care

"Yours are good and strong," she says.
"They should, with proper care, last
a lifetime. Now open just a little
wider, won't you?" Proper is the operative
word here. She has part of each hand
in my mouth, cat's cradle with a single
strand. "Good and strong," she croons, but
I feel it coming, worked down hard between
teeth to bleeding gums because (she says this
gently) "you don't do it enough yourself."

There is something of the honest
used car dealer in her tone, vaguely admonishing
against unnecessary expense. I want to reply
but she's in to the wrists now. She breaks
a strand between the second and third molar,
curses softly and rearms, flexing it before her
like piano wire. "Who did that work in there?"
she demands. "There's no room between the teeth."

"Who?" she asks again, flexing the wire, testing
my allegiances. "Dr. Hammer," I say, a joke I expect
a hygienist will appreciate, one whose punch line
happens to be true. But she's humorless, back at it
with the renewed fervor of a true believer. Suddenly
I'm terrified, my mouth stretched like a mask
of tragedy. "He's dead now," I manage to gasp
between withdrawals. "Uh huh," she hums,
distracted by something now, back in
to the windpipe. "I can imagine," she says.

Delayed at Sea-Tac

Six hours later the woman at the counter
doesn't know anything about it. At four a.m.
coffee and Bloody Marys are free—little cakes
sealed in cellophane. It is the least
they can do. They do it.

No matter how they reroute you, the luggage
will catch up. You imagine bags, locked
and leather, hoofing it cross-country—
east of Butte somewhere, tangled in barbed wire,
confused by cattle still in their skins.

The intercom says, "We regret this temporary
delay." You consider that, wonder if, by definition,
all delays aren't temporary. You listen to ice
melt in your glass. At the little cart you recall
standing, taking the ten steps across.

"Could I get just one more?" A new girl is on.
She looks up and smiles her whole salary.

Changing Names

There is no sound of water.
You've nailed the river
to its stones.
This dream is so real
you can't stop living it.

The night opens
like a lizard's mouth
and you slide down in.
You wake to dark so deep
it becomes someone else's silence.

Try out the name
you feel on your tongue.
It sounds almost right.
Try again and it's closer.
The river pulls free.

If you wake at night and feel
something near, a hand almost touching
inside your own, roll over and listen.
There is the sound the river makes
rehearsing all our names.

Listening Through Smoke

Back from Munich at the blunt end of a weekend,
I sit in the *Stiegl Ecke* opposite the Salzburg *Bahnhof*,
waiting in the smoke for beer and local soup, a bus
to wind me back into the mountains. I live up there

among mountains with names as lovely and remote
to me as the village women. It's clear now, listening
through smoke to the others, how far removed
understanding is from proper pronunciation.

In German my expectations are tempered by ignorance—
the poor man's humility. I speak a little but cannot
understand. Now, in the smoke, it occurs to me
I have the same trouble with English.

When I think of the problems I've had
with possessive pronouns, the conditional,
the future perfect. The past is hopeless, the present
too limited to express the range of my desires.

As for German, what little known is lost
in the Austrian dialect, a subtle rounding, contracting
of the language that varies village to village, expressive
of regional pride and a smoldering hatred toward Germany.

I close my eyes and listen through the smoke.
I catch the verbs "to need," "to want," "to believe,"
then imagine my own voice smoothed, rounded,
local, behind which something else is being said.

The waitress brings me beer and soup. She knows
my fatigue by her own. All of us are waiting
for something. For forty schillings the bus will take us
somewhere, but it cannot bring us home.

These Leaves, This Light

These leaves, damp as the belly
of a snail, grip the cobbles
turning wet on Bartensteingasse
in a fine mist falling.

This light through the window is memory
lifting its tired face again. I am wearied
by a life so weighted with received desire
I can barely drag it with me.

Around the corner a tram rails by, reminds
me this is not my neighborhood, this is not
my country. Only the leaves seem familiar.
I drain the last amber light from the glass,

pay what I owe and step outside. Am I
really lost? I board a tram running straight
as a spoke to the woods. I carry
hunger with me like a map.

She Says It Lingers

—for K, at the death of her father

She says it lingers
into sky, disperses the way
clouds will, without any overall loss
of water in the cycle. She seems certain
the soul will reaccumulate later and fall again

the way rain will
sprinkle the parched tongue
of a summer field, or as snow dusts
an argued landscape when something suddenly
changes. No one dies, exactly. They evaporate into

a pure kind of smoke.
It burns the eyes, she says,
and weeps. Outside in the world
our train rushes through, a little boy
stands by a gate to a deep green field and waves.

The Crows Leave Vienna

1.

You crows, three winters I've listened
to the sometimes actual words you make
when wind mixes the rubbing of magnolia limbs
with your own rough syntax—a language

cold drives from the Russian Steppes
each fall to these freshly harvested vineyards.
But neglected grapes are not enough
to sustain an appetite I begin to understand

is more complicated. In exchange for lessons,
I throw old bread through my kitchen window
while it is still too dark for the neighbors to complain.
The couple who live below are in on it too.

From them I learned the disturbing truth
of your appetite for meat. I rhymed the clatter
of a window closing with your sudden frenzied leap
from the tiered magnolia limbs—an almost

rabid enthusiasm the like of which my own
stale offerings do not occasion. How you lunge
and thrust your ruthless beaks among the ungleaned
bones below! What hunger of mine compares?

2.

You crows, now I've found you out. All winter
you lift above the houses in great black waves
of wind, clouds of living darkness out of which
the snow itself seems to fall. Yours is the uneducated

yawp Whitman wanted to believe was his own.
I've watched the black river you make of the sky
without ever hoping to know where you were going.
But now my friend comes home with news

of your whereabouts. She visits men dying there
of the world's most popular plague, housed
with their fellows in a building so beautiful
the city must be loathe to move them later.

You roost there in your thousands, singing the dark
door open. Rib of our rib, you call at the gate of the viscera
for what this world no longer wants. In this you love
most thoroughly, lacking for once even a hint of irony.

As with any display of unasked honesty, we stagger
among your multitudes, eyes averted, terrified some
untoward move of ours will send your roiling cowl
flapping into our crafted world—each dark shard

insisting its cryptic syllable, a blistering cacophony
that resolves itself into a promise only the dying understand:
All that sloughs away, you say, *will find its final home
with us. We will show your hunger how to find the sky.*

After Differences

1.

The candle holds its tongue
to my throat and I rise, wavering
in my own heat. The cut stem of the rose
leans from the water glass and the door
stays slammed.

Night leans on the window. A single rose
is no bouquet, but water does what it can,
climbing the stem from habit
as the sun will the sky when we are all gone.
No harm in that. But for now the world is dark.

2.

Morning traffic is a moving bruise, sound made angry
by so much past tense. I stir beside you, but already
you are missing. A tram rails by. Your robe
flutters the half open door, and it closes.

3.

Light crosses the table between us.
Beyond the window a cloud of crows
disperses like ashes over the winter city.
I hear them calling one to the other.
You and I say nothing. This could be

our lives—moments sloughed away
like flecks of dry skin. A red petal
droops from the rose in the glass,
the lower lip of someone lost
in thought and staring out the window.

A Rose for Bunnell

Life jumps from the bat. Bunnell whirls and runs
for the fence. We are speechless. Our shoes are laced
with words. He lets it fall like a ripe plum, takes it easy
over his shoulder in deep left center and rifles it
flat as a punch line for home.

Things change. All chances are the same chance
until you take your pick—then the future shuffles
and resettles like the board at the *Bahnhof*
when one train pulls in and another pulls out.
In Amsterdam I looked out the window to you waving
in the gray light. But it was you who were leaving.

Ah, old friend, in the end lets enjoy what dessert
brings to the table. The main course fades to this
final sweetness: The game is lately over. A woman
in black crosses the green field. Birds linger in the circle
of trees that surround us. It is springtime because we need
these beginnings. We're alive. Anything can happen.

Separation

"If you want perspective, emphasize distance—
resolutely widen the lines that converge on the horizon."
                                        —*Paul Gauguin*

To begin, I trace the long thin line
of the horizon, then choose a point
beyond which I imagine you
disappearing. Bear in mind your importance

in these calculations. Every distance holds
to its point of reference. The same is true
of separation, which owes itself finally
to attachment. Simple facts contain us.

By this measure I map out my boundaries.
Only a few names and all my limitations
are made real. I hold the depth of my vision
to the circle around me. You are located

relative to the missing, a point fixed
to your name. And yet at night when the stars
reel toward you, I dream I hear you singing.
What worlds can you see, looking away?

Freundlicher Alptraum

I don't know him, but in the dream
we're old friends. He's brushing his teeth
in the Frankfurt *Bahnhof*. We seem to live there
along that passage where wet winter light rises
into the financial district. He grins into a slab
of glass above a row of smeared white sinks.

Time has passed. He's walking away
along an empty curve of underground track
with almost nothing left in his mouth.
It presents like a film sequence, one we've reshot
so often it has made of the hypothetical an insinuation
of reality. He says, "You'd want your mouth empty
at a moment like this." His tone is matter-of-fact, almost
patronizing. The words are a train, the way they slide

around the corner, as though they've been always
on their way. They seem so final, so nonnegotiable.
He is perfectly clean, walking toward the slice
of yellow light arcing against the black curve
of tunnel wall, just walking, his mouth
empty—not a word left inside it, nothing
but teeth, so clean, so perfect.

Winter Garden

Some mornings a face passes
in a tram window going the other way,
or a leaf falls past my bedroom window,
while outside the old man from next door
works his rake beneath the bushes, and along
the fence the first spring flowers push through.

What live coal have I banked against my own
fear of winter? I am rigid with worry, ready
to snap in the lightest breeze. Then a face
goes by the other way. The old man works
in the garden, and sunlight through the limbs
of the yew tree scatters shadows among the small

yellow blossoms marked off with sticks.
All winter the old man knows just where
not to put his foot down. Now with the flowers
speaking for themselves, he moves slowly
through the garden, pulling up stakes
and dropping them into a deep white pail.

Failed Poet Grading Vocabulary Quizzes

He staggers the fields of January, trailing blood,
circling every deviant use as though to throw himself
off his own trail. He knows the white wolf
is behind him somewhere—on the blind side

of that last copse of sycamores, or beyond
the frozen river one valley further south—
nose to the blood spoor and as patient
as a broken promise. The man feels a victim
of the accident his life has become. He believes

in the kind of loss that requires complicity—
the gradual bleeding away of ironies
and his old ability to enter the wolf himself
and relentlessly track them down. He waits
in the glare of the desk lamp too late at night

looking back across empty white fields
the way he knows it must come. A murder
of crows careens there in winter wind
above bone-bare trees. He wonders whether
they are aware of the cold, there is so much

of joy in their movements. While he watches
he lets that sudden white blur enter his field
of vision from the left. He wants it to end
this way, watching the crows. The wolf gathers
himself at the blurred end of a long sprint

and leaps. He strikes the snow and wheels
without blood on his fangs. There is nothing
there to attack. His own tracks have refused

to follow him. On the field's clean edge
he sees the crows drift down to the snow.

They shuffle and nudge and otherwise dance,
restless, hungry, and real.

Returning the Wolf

The news all week in Boise has been
the return of the wolf to the middle fork
of the Salmon River—The River of No Return—
a government airlift from Alberta
through the foggy skies of talk show hype,
threats from ranchers, the hysterical
telling of a tale from northern Minnesota
where Little Red Ridinghood has apparently been
swallowed all over again. Last night I dreamt

I was running uphill from our childhood
swimming hole, making tracks across the dunes
to where waves urged all night against one edge
of the world. Then the hill undid itself into a road
above Coos Bay. A man in a school bus insisted

I ride. We swerved into traffic on the *Hauptstrasse*
running through Salzburg to the train station. The wolf
ran wild-eyed in front of us, trapped in traffic, slipping
on a cold clear sheet of ice. I jumped from the bus
and gathered her up. We were caught in Coos Bay
again, the hillsides scabby with clearcuts. I dodged
through thickets of pickups and chip trucks, desperate
for any unpaved chance at the hills. She ran beside me

now along a forest road above the vineyards
at *Neustift am Walde*. In the woods near Vienna
I found myself familiar. "I know the way," I shouted.
She threw me a glance, all wolf grin and steaming
smile. Moonlight through bare sycamore limbs
cast down shapes from fairytales. The world blurred.

We were in Salzburg again. I held a compass
out in front of her, showed the four directions.

She swallowed me. I had them inside. All terror
and desire, I dodged among headlights, felt
my paws lose grip and slid along my side
into the *Salzach*. Water rushed from the world's mouth.
I reached the other side and shed the river, running uphill
in the moonlight—no howl, no headlights—alone.

Consciousness

*"Consciousness is energy
striving to become aware of itself."*

We studied it for years. My professor
was a Marxist, his voice as beautiful
and monotonous as his circumscribed
philosophy. I was not a believer, so I

listened instead to the tone of that voice,
riding it day after comfortable day
into waning afternoon light without
ever attending to the actual words.

It became in this way my own voice, my own
actuality. And now my own students ride it, nodding
and pleasant, untroubled by content, into a world
that has no more use for Marx.

Like the face my mother said would set that way
if I didn't unmake it, I have almost succeeded
in becoming what I must have seemed to be.
As for consciousness, I have only this to say.

Wolf Reverb

I huff and I puff, but the house
stays right there. Straw and sticks
give strength to bricks. These three
little piggies are too well diversified.
If the market demands change, then
maybe a taste of Granny will do.

What she believes the world is
will set the door ajar—this basket,
my little-girl self. The hungry woman
she never let herself be
went skipping down the lane
and comes a-knocking back in me.

Ah, the brittle bones lean forward—
low-cal, curious, fat-free.
"My dear," she says, "what a big need
you have!" When I smile, my eye teeth
wink and evaluate. "It's the piggies," I say.
"So pink, so plump and misleading."

Object Lesson

The only thing I really know of wine—
how to tilt the glass and let that crafted darkness

run inside. I sit now on the edge of the bed,
already an old man, and try to find my way back
into the story night has offered. But morning

gathers itself in the empty limbs of the maple
beyond the window, its yellowed leaves
thick and wet on the garden floor.

Daylight Savings

In a dream you are about to wake from,
a long chase sequence ends with a joke
made by a man just caught by the others—
his entire family about to be slaughtered.

The man—both father and son—is no one
you know. Bravado does not quite cover
the matter-of-fact tone of the man and his son
trapped in a one room body, the rest of the family

implied by context. His joke addresses the shirtless
man dusted with a fine white powder evocative
of cave paint. The quip—some reference to luminosity—
is already lost like his name. Details sink like clear water running

into sand. You cannot pluck him from kaleidoscopic stretches
of imagery. The relevant characters file into the killing room,
particulars already fading into the blank face of an almost
beautiful woman, her features made up just past credibility,

shoulder angled against a darkness gathering all of us now.

Dark Matter

No surprise here: darkness has mass, has light
on its back foot. We are made of the obvious
observations every child already imagined.
The universe is a closet door left slightly

ajar. The space beneath the bed breeds
galaxies. Light is heat conjured at the edge
of nothing, a necessary but conjectured
condition bounded by shadow. Consider

the terrible gap between intentions
and the multifarious realities that explode
from each, the meant and the unmeant
leapfrogging in directionless abandon.

We impose order to find a place
to stand, the cave mouth hanging agape,
its spark of light silhouetting us
against the absolute expanse of night.

Home Made

I believe in the generative clarity
of first places. In the twisted limbs of shorepine
I see what the wind's been doing. The dunes

shrug their long blond shoulders
into the creek, a beaver slaps the dark
beneath the willows. Winter rain
sorts through my father's ashes.

Conundrums

In this case, point of view is everything.
The question of the tree falling in the forest
focuses on the wrong point entirely, confusing
the empirical logic of science with imagination.
The first owes everything to the second, despite
what they may try to tell you.

If there is no one in the forest to hear
the tree fall, who's to say there is a forest?
If we are willing to imagine the clever man's
forest, shouldn't we extend the courtesy
to the sound of the falling tree?

Only the deaf man is spared this logic.
He might say, "I can't hear you,"
and there we would be, left standing
in a forest of our own making,
the tree's soundless fall
our hypothetical hearts stopping.

The Woodpecker

—for Dorothy, in memory of Bill Stafford

It is hard to imagine
birds dying, though I have
from time to time
found one on its side, already
as hollow as its bones.

I don't mean killed
by cats or the unpracticed aim
of boys auditioning their first .22,
but dying of what's called natural
causes, as though the redundant instincts
of us domesticates no longer apply.

It is the woodpecker,
powdered red head tapping
at the holly tree, that occasions this—
the way he ignores the clusters of red berries
that make the clumsy robins drunk
and hammers instead a uniform line
of holes through the tough gray bark.

Once he's flown, I enter
the wet light beyond the window
to read the lines of Braille
his patient hunger left behind. In the rain,
the damp bark beneath my fingers
looses a shuddering sorrow
at the thought of his passing.

Dream of Winter Water

A boy and an old man stand
on a winter river bank separated
by distances hard to account for.

Downstream in the belly of a bend
the old man stands among willows
and looks back upstream at the boy.

The boy has seen something in the water
and wants to tell someone. He raises
a hand and shouts. The gesture, a sudden

thrust of his hand into listless sky, already
seems habitual. The man rubs his shoulder
absently. The boy is pointing at something

now, his shouts lost in the churl of water
undermining the bank beneath the old
man's feet. He knows without looking

what the boy sees. He lets the bank
soften beneath him. The boy has turned
away now and disappears into shore pine

and salal with an incoherent story forgotten
before he bursts through the back door
into the silence of an empty house.

Summer Solstice, Newport Beach

This is the last day
of my forty-sixth year.
I've spent the morning
being fitted for glasses.
It seems I can no longer see
what is right in front of me.

At the edge of the patio
ants pass one another in a seemingly
endless coming and going.
Upstairs my mother-in-law
speaks in desperately upbeat tones
to someone on the phone. My wife
naps in the next room, our first child
unfurling inside her like tentative
new growth at the edge of summer.

Jets from John Wayne roar one
after another above the mudflats
of the back bay, while beneath them
mud-colored birds hunt the tidal edges.
Today lasts longer than all the others.
They get shorter and shorter after this.

Hunter Gatherer

—Balboa Island, June 2012

On the morning walk to Starbucks for two blonde
drips and the boy's bagel, severed hydrangea blossoms
litter the street corner of Amethyst like crumpled tissues
cast off by a consumptive outpatient. The marine layer
is a gauzy blanket drawn to the fevered chin of the mainland.
Colorado burns; the heartland swelters. Florida suffers another
tropical depression. Unseasonal rain in the Northwest.

The line at the coffee shop is out the door as always.
Short shorts in Nikes jitters in front of me; an original
cinnamon roll dangles from her off-hand like low hanging
fruit within reach of Tantalus. A froth white Lexus idles
at the curb. Down the flag-lined street, a rising tide
laps the containment wall circling the island.

Sanctimony is the thin coat I wear against such weather.
I drop a can in the proper bin and limit my use of plastic.
I was born to paucity then grew into excess. My own
two children are likely to travel that road in reverse. Is this
where poetry meets justice? There's no grudge, no sense
of right or wrong. Just me, making my way home past blossoms
wilting in the street, hands full of warmth and goodness.

Ring Finger

Tonight arthritis in my ring finger
reminds me of all the good fortune
I can't quite get a grip on. This

illegal fire on the hill above the house
leaps through the dead limbs of winter
blow down fed by our two children

dragging them from the field. They
laugh and shriek their perfect names
at each other, vying to leverage

the biggest limb into the blaze. Here
is where love and memory begin—
all the deadfall of winter cured

to red slash and fed into the dangerous
heat. Laughter is an orange tongue of light
living in this swarm of sparks and stars.

Lecture on Emptiness

My wife no longer wants to hear from me
on this, how the emptiness of take-out coffee
cups or suitcases in even the best series or film
suggests a more pervasive hollowness. Method
actors pretending to sip hot liquids from obviously

empty cups unmasks a world bereft of surface
tension. It violates the necessary suspension
of disbelief upon which all such versions
of vicarious truth depend. Vacations taken with
empty bags in tow depress me in the same way

those drinks decorated with paper umbrellas may
mock the irksome myth of privilege and plenty
in actual life, though this, it seems, is just a garden
variety failure of unintended irony—a bit like
a voice-over track applied to clarify the obvious.

But let's return to the physics of emptiness, the necessity
of weight and its relationship to gravity. Jesse Pinkman
offers a welcome counterclaim, the weight of his duffle
bag bulked with bundled hundreds pulling him down
as he muscles it past empty-eyed meth heads gaping

at the flat screen his ill-gotten largesse has bought him.
This, it seems, is how allegory should actually
work, the suggestion of weight in service of the emptiness
that radiates from its own gravitational center, pulling
all the necessary consequences into orbit around it. Here

mass is exaggerated to underscore its own antithesis—
the ineluctable relationship between action and its
downstream implications—a resonant, weighty emptiness
burdened with made choices. Here at last is hollowness
we can celebrate, its heat real and dangerous to the touch.

String Theory

This seven-month-old banging his spoon
against a plate in the café seems gifted
to his parents. They no longer recognize
themselves sitting at all the other tables
maybe eighteen months before, trying
to smile indulgently and scanning the room
for empty tables further afield.

Indeed, when they look in any mirror—
not just these at the far end of the room—
they scarcely recognize the strangers
looking back. Somewhere that other world
must still exist, perhaps spread out around
the couple in the corner, the young woman
gripping the knuckled hands of her man, hissing
some urgent message over the salt cellar.

Meanwhile, in this one, *Goodnight Moon,* already
worn at the corners, peaks from the heavy
canvas bag into which a nippled bottle
of breast milk is stowed. The limp-eyed
mother shoulders all of it while father lifts his
prodigy aloft and makes for the door, universal
applause implied by the silence.

Passion in Winter

In the garden, the broken necks
of sunflowers hang their ungainly heads
pecked empty. I work a shovel beneath
the roots of rotten stalks and let them fall.

The hunger of birds consoles me.
They eat what there is and seem satisfied.
I feel calmed by gray skies and molding leaves
beneath these empty trees. In the scribble
of weeds and blackberry vines below
the garden, the wilderness waits.

Coyotes come down from the ragged angles
of clearcuts below Mount Hood. They sing
into that darkness where the fields give way
to suburbs just east of the city. This is our life.
In winter, the face of the planet turns just slightly
away from the light—a man by a reading lamp
pausing to look out into the dark beyond the window,
unsure what it is that has distracted his attention.

Tumor

He is not a child
I know
but because my little boy
runs laughing down the hallway
and into my arms,
I know him.

I know his father
is an old friend of my wife
and that she too knows
both little boys
and how they run toward you
in good dreams
and bad.

I see her knowing.
I see them running
toward us and away
and know that this is
all love ever was and so
I open my arms and let it
run laughing into them.

This is what we can do.
This is all we can ever do.

Valley of the Shadow

So my mother calls the other night.
In December she turns ninety
and has to take an eye test to keep
her license. She suffers from macular

degeneration and has not driven
after dark for several years. She gets
shots in each eye every few months
to stave off total blindness. She admits

to being a little nervous about this
test. She lives in rural Oregon, and without
a license she loses her ability to live
independently. I think you can see

where this is going. Last week a man stepped out
into a shadow in front of her car. Enough light
gathered inside her to activate the brake. This
jaywalker is still walking, unaware of what darkness

might have made of his assumptions, and my mother,
a believing Catholic, takes light and shadow beyond
literal iterations into a complex realm
of perceptual uncertainties. She sees a chart

in front of her that reveals even the largest shapes
as blurred by time, a familiar path through the woods
after the sun has fallen. You feel this world reliably
beneath your feet. Memory claims this is the way to go.

Believe it. Just a little further now.

Scotchbroom

—for my father

Like us, it's a latecomer,
opportunistic, willing to take
what's left. It offers poor soils
a nitrogen fix, the minimum wage
of primary cover, then smothers them
in their own dependency.

It borrows the wind and the hunger
of birds, hitchhikes the drafts of chip trucks
blowing down highways to the next new place.
It follows loggers into clearcuts
and farmers into fields that won't stay cleared.

Each spring it gives the sky a shout
of yellow blossoms. Entire hillsides blaze
with a coward's color until we relent
and call them beautiful.

Think of the struggle you and I have had
with it—the grudging respect that follows
failure. Younger, I've favored pulling it
by the roots, a dictum you offered
when you believed your back would last
forever. Your willingness later to mow it
at ground level I viewed as abdication.

I bend my knees and lift with all of myself,
but those that endure take root for good
reason and flower in air they've earned.
We own at last what we can't be rid of.

Sixty-One

Somewhere Stafford called the sun
the one star that loves us, though
I doubt he thought that himself.
He spoke of one syllable suggesting
the next, a sort of sibilant sequencing
of sound before meaning interposes.

Six decades completed. What to show.
My mother is sitting in a chair just there,
ninety-one, sipping morning coffee,
front door open, traffic passing
on 101 just beyond the trees. She believes
the sun loves us by shining, evidence

everywhere rising from the ground. I don't
see it that way; flowers and limbs turn
toward the light as faces turn to the popular
boy in class who later disappoints with his
indifference. He is Stevens' necessary
angel, there because without him there is

only absence, six line stanzas without form
or meaning, six decades stretching out behind
me, my mother three ahead, falling to sleep
now, scouting the terrain in advance, showing me
without meaning to what kind of love shines
from above, what kind of purpose I may find.

Dispersal of Ashes

"Do you want me to sing
you a song?" my father asked
the last time I talked with him.

His voice was faraway—
more than two continents
and an ocean between us.

He said, "I'm looking out the window
at R.T. and Robert. They think they know
how to lay in a crop. I'm about to go out there
and show them what's what."

These were brothers, estranged
and long dead—still boys
in the wide Nebraska fields
he'd left after the war for Oregon.

"Why don't you wait?" I said.
"I'm headed your way."

He came back for me then.
I heard him breathing—how he tried
to catch his breath.

"You're not headed
where I'm headed," he said.
He laughed about that.
And then he began
to sing.

Resolve

We have peculiar needs. We believe
in beginnings, fresh starts, the low numbers
on the calendar. We love a countdown
and know numbers as facts one by one
discarded. The sloughed skin of our days
sets the future free.

Hunger too is a kind of beginning—desire
with teeth added for the pragmatist.
Breathe on a relief map and it whispers
that direction is chance augmented
by ocean currents, wind patterns, rainfall,
faith in the politics of seed dispersal—
all complicated by the beast that asks why.

Outside my window, crows arrange themselves
around the last wrinkled apple on a new year's limb.
There's no need for diligence, hunger has such
an unfailing memory. The core invites the beak
to it. A fading chain of summers lingers there,
an ovoid willingness suspended in a pulp
of old light—seeds as dark about the core
as are the birds black around the apple.

One by one these crows drop into the wind,
in their gullets the seed that passes for life.
The earth gives of its groaning goodness
while we flap away into sharded darkness
full of such meager news: Fruit is more
than fruit. Hunger is not what it seems.
Words are made of edges and hollows
the wind blows through until we hear a song.

Acknowledgments

Grateful acknowledgement is made to the editors of the following publications in which earlier versions of some of these poems first appeared:

Alaska Quarterly Review: "Winter Garden," "Thumbnail Sketch," and "Dark Matter"

American Poetry Review: "Lecture on Emptiness" *(forthcoming)*

The Fishtrap Anthology: "Home Made"

Fireweed: "A Rose for Bunnell," "To Sharpen a Pulaski," and "Listening Through Smoke"

Northwest Review: "Managed Care"

Poetry Northwest: "Changing Names," "Delayed at Sea-Tac," "Conundrums," "Failed Poet Grading Vocabulary Quizzes," "Returning the Wolf," *"pinus contorta,"* "Separations," "Saying a World," and "The Woodpecker"

The Seattle Review: "Wolf Reverb"

Talus and Scree: "After Differences"

Voices In Winter Rain: "Scotchbroom"

West Wind Review: "Not Writing Friends"

Wildfire: "To Sharpen a Pulaski" (reprinted by permission)

"Changing Names" also appeared in the Australian journal *Overland.*

"Not Writing Friends" won *West Wind Review's* 1987 poetry contest.

Many of these poems, sometimes in earlier versions, appeared in the chapbook *The Clever Man's Forest,* Traprock Books, 2011.

I am indebted to many people. First and foremost I wish to thank Michael McGriff for his friendship and his tireless advocacy of this work. Special thanks are owed to Dorianne Laux for selecting the manuscript and to Rodger Moody for his selfless efforts to shape that manuscript into this book. I wish to offer special thanks to David Wagoner, whom I have never met, for his generous attention to my work over the years at *Poetry Northwest*. His acceptances gave me confidence at critical times.

Special thanks also to Erik Muller for his work on *The Clever Man's Forest*, and the crucial impetus it brought in its wake. His generous spirit is a gift to Oregon poetry.

Among my many teachers I wish especially to thank John Noland, Erik Muller, Vern Rutsala, Gary Miranda, C.D. Wright, Michael Harper, and Keith Waldrop. My deepest gratitude is owed to Dr. John Callahan at Lewis and Clark College, whose passionate support of my early work opened the doors to the Graduate Writer's Workshop at Brown University.

For their friendship, their art, their inspiration, their kindness, I wish to thank Bill Stafford, Kim Stafford, Michael Ford, Paulann Petersen, Matthew Dickman, Carl Adamshick, Natalie Garyet, Jim Thurber, Jeff Wallach, Roby Roberts, and Lael Pinney. Finally, for their patience and unending forbearance, I wish to thank my students, my colleagues, and especially my wife, Jan, and our two children, Branson and Delaney.

Notes

"Winter Garden" is dedicated to the memory of Bill Stafford.

"Ring Finger" is for Jan, as is "Lecture on Emptiness."

"Lecture on Emptiness": Jesse Pinkman is Walter White's hapless foil in *Breaking Bad*.

"To Sharpen a Pulaski": A pulaski is a tool used by firefighters, its head half ax and half grubbing hoe.

"Separations": The epigram from Gauguin was suggested to me by C. D. Wright; the poem is dedicated to her memory.

"*Freundlicher Alptraum*": Thanks to my student, Luiza Fischleder, for consultation on this title, which translates roughly as "*Friendly Nightmare.*"

"Daddy Leaves Home" is for Mary Brunette.

"The Crows Leave Vienna" is in memory of Christian Wild, Uli Landauer, and Theo Stefansky.

"Passion in Winter" is dedicated to the memory of Gary Britton.

"To Sharpen a Pulaski" and "Thumbnail Sketch" are for Rebecca Wilson.

"A Rose for Bunnell" is for Tim Bunnell.

"Returning the Wolf" is for Jim and Nina Cook.

"Conundrums" is for Joseph Monninger.

About the Author

PHOTO BY LEX THOMPSON

Robert Hunter Jones spent three years as a logger in the Oregon Coast Range and two years working the swing shift in a sawmill in his hometown of Lakeside, Oregon, before returning to college to study literature and writing. After attending Southwestern Oregon Community College in Coos Bay, he won a scholarship to complete his undergraduate degree at Lewis and Clark College and, subsequently, a Fellowship to the Graduate Writing Program at Brown University. Jones worked for eight seasons on National Park Service fire crews, five at Crater Lake National Park, where he did research on fire effects and fire suppression, and three seasons with Arrowhead Hotshots, a type one fire crew based in Sequoia/Kings Canyon National Park. He published a series of essays in *Wild Earth* and *Wildfire Magazine* arguing for the return of fire to wilderness ecosystems and the need to reshape the role of professional wildland firefighters to meet the challenges posed by a century of widespread fire suppression. His poetry has appeared, or is forthcoming, in *Alaska Quarterly Review, American Poetry Review, Cumberland Poetry Review, Fireweed, Northwest Review, Poetry Northwest, Seattle Review,* and *West Wind Review*, among others, and in the chapbook *The Clever Man's Forest*, Traprock Books, 2011. Since 1990 he has taught Literature and Theory of Knowledge at American International School of Vienna, in Vienna, Austria, where he lives with his wife and two children.

The interior text and display type as well as the back cover text were set in Adobe Jenson, a faithful electronic version of the 1470 roman face of Nicolas Jenson. Jenson was a Frenchman employed as the mintmaster at Tours. Legend has it that he was sent to Mainz in 1458 by Charles VII to learn the new art of printing in the shop of Gutenberg, and import it to France. But he never returned, appearing in Venice in 1468; there his first roman types appeared, in his edition of Eusebius. He moved to Rome at the invitation of Pope Sixtus IV, where he died in 1480.

Type historian Daniel Berkeley Updike praises the Jenson Roman for "its readability, its mellowness of form, and the evenness of color in mass." Updike concludes, "Jenson's roman types have been the accepted models for roman letters ever since he made them, and, repeatedly copied in our own day, have never been equalled."

The typeface used on the front cover and spine is Legato. Designed for legibility, its essential attribute is that the black of the individual letterforms is made equal in importance to the white inside and between the letters. By making the black and white harmonize, Legato approaches an ideal of readability, since reading involves the perception of positive/negative space as one thing.

Silverfish Review Press is committed to preserving ancient forests and natural resources. We elected to print *Winter Garden* on 30% post consumer recycled paper, processed chlorine free. As a result, for this printing, we have saved: 1 tree (40′ tall and 6-8″ diameter), 499 gallons of water, 293 kilowatt hours of electricity, 64 pounds of solid waste, and 120 pounds of greenhouse gases. Thomson-Shore, Inc. is a member of Green Press Initiative, a nonprofit program dedicated to supporting authors, publishers, and suppliers in their efforts to reduce their use of fiber obtained from endangered forests. For more information, visit www.greenpressinitiative.org.

Cover design by Valerie Brewster, Scribe Typography
Text design by Rodger Moody and Connie Kudura, ProtoType
Printed on acid-free papers and bound by Thomson-Shore, Inc.